CPSIA information can be obtained
at www.ICGtesting.com
Printed in the USA
BVHW011615170519
548609BV00012B/677/P